TPL Dataflow by Example

Dataflow and Reactive Programming in .Net

Matt Carkci

TPL Dataflow by Example

Dataflow and Reactive Programming in .Net

Matt Carkci

This book is for sale at http://DataflowBook.com

This version was published on 2014-05-29

ISBN 978-1499149357

Contents

Other Dataflow Books

In depth coverage of Dataflow and Reactive Programming including:

- Sample code for three styles of reactive programming systems with chapters that explain their operations
- Summaries of Flow Based Programming, the Actor Model and Communicating Sequential Processes (CSP)
- Explanation of all features found in reactive systems

Visit http://DataflowBook.com for more information

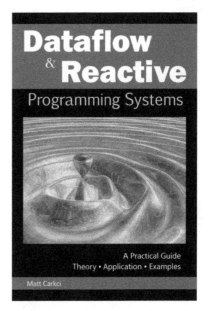

Dataflow and Reactive Programming Systems

Code Examples

All of the code in this book can be
downloaded from ftp://DataflowBook.com.

Visit http://DataflowBook.com for more information
and blog posts about dataflow and reactive programming.

Contact the author at matt@deepFriedCode.com

1 Getting Started

1.1 What is TPL Dataflow

The TPL Dataflow Library (also called TDF) is built on top of the existing Task Parallel Library (TPL). It allows you to easily create parallel applications without worrying about low-level details by implementing a time tested programming model called "Dataflow."

1.2 What is Dataflow

Dataflow is about the movement of data. It stands in contrast to "control-flow" which is used in most mainstream programming languages like C# and Visual Basic. The common control-flow statements like "if" and "for" loops do not exist in dataflow. Instead, it is the data that determines how the program executes.

Dataflow consists of "blocks" and "links". A block is a container for code and a link transfers data from one block to another. Blocks also have inputs to receive data and outputs to send data. Think of a block as a function whose arguments are the inputs and whose return value is the output of the block.

When a block has data on its input, it will consume the data and pass it to the internal function. The result of the function is then placed on the block's output. If the output of the block is connected to the input of another block, the data is sent along the link to the input of the next block and the process starts all over again.

The key point to understand is that it's the data arriving at a block's input that causes it to execute. The programmer doesn't need to specifically poll the input to see if data is available. The block reacts to the existence of data. That is why the term "Reactive Programming" has been used for decades to describe dataflow.

1.3 Where is Dataflow Used?

Dataflow excels in three areas:

- Processing streams of data
- Parallelization
- Reacting to changing data

In any domain where streams of data are essential, dataflow can represent the program much more directly than our common, imperative programming techniques. Audio and video processing are two common examples.

Even if you are not dealing with data streams, dataflow can still make asynchronous processes easier to build by handling the threading issues. Microprocessor speeds are not increasing like they did from 1980s to 2000s. But we are getting more cores per chip. The problem has always been the difficulty of handling asynchronous computations combined with mutable state. Dataflow encapsulates the state inside of the blocks while the channels between blocks are the only dependencies.

Dataflow is also starting to take over batch processing of "big data." Instead of running a nightly batch, dataflow programs allow for real-time analysis of the data.

Recently a new term has become popular, Reactive Programming. While dataflow has been described as reactive for long time, currently programmers use the term to mean a better way to handle event-driven programming without callbacks. Microsoft's Reactive Extensions lead this resurgence of dataflow.

1.4 TPL Dataflow vs. Rx

The Reactive Extensions (Rx) are for managing a stream of events by using standard LINQ operations while TPL Dataflow is adept at handling streams of any type of data.

1.5 Installing TPL Dataflow

TPL Dataflow is distributed separately from the .Net Framework. Currently there are official versions for .Net versions 4.5 and 3.5. For .Net 4.0 there is an unofficial port from the Mono project but I have not tested it.

The recommended way to download the library is through NuGet although it is also possible to download it directly from the Microsoft website.

2 TPL Dataflow Basics

2.1 Blocks

In dataflow, blocks (or nodes) are entities that may send and receive data and are the basic unit of composition. The TPL Dataflow Library comes with a handful of predefined blocks, while they're very basic, they should cover 99% of your needs. Using these predefined blocks, you can build your own application specific blocks.

Think of the predefined blocks as being equivalent to keywords in C#. You build C# applications by using the keywords. The predefined blocks similarly define the basic operations of dataflow programs that you use to build your dataflow application.

Of the predefined blocks offered by the TPL Dataflow library, we can categorize them into three groups, blocks that process data (execution blocks), blocks that buffer or store data (buffer blocks) and blocks that group data together into collections (grouping blocks). In the follow sections we'll examine each category of block and discover how they work with simple code examples.

2.1.1 Execution Blocks

Execution blocks process data very similar to how methods accept data and possibly returns a value. At creation you pass either a `Func` or an `Action` that defines what the execution block will do with the data.

All execution blocks contain an internal buffer that defaults to an unbounded capacity.

2.1.1.1 ActionBlock<T>

An `ActionBlock<T>` has a single input and no output. It is used when you need to do something with the input data but won't need to pass it along to other blocks. It is the equivalent to the `Action<T>` class. In dataflow, this type of block is often called a "sink" because the data sinks into it like a black hole, never to emerge again.

At creation, an `ActionBlock<T>` accepts an `Action<T>` that is called when data arrives at the input.

An internal buffer is present on the input of an `ActionBlock<T>`. The buffer defaults to an unbounded capacity but this can be changed by using `DataflowBlockOptions` mentioned later.

ActionBlock<T> Example 1

Basic usage, Block threading, Post()

```
1    using System;
2    using System.Threading.Tasks.Dataflow;
3
4    namespace TPLDataflowByExample
5    {
6        static class ActionBlockExample1
7        {
8            static public void Run() {
9
10               var actionBlock = new ActionBlock<int>(n => Console.WriteLine(n));
11
12               for (int i = 0; i < 10; i++) {
13                   actionBlock.Post(i);
14               }
15
16               Console.WriteLine("Done");
17           }
18       }
19   }
```

This example shows the basic usage of an `ActionBlock<T>` and how to send data to all types of blocks that accept inputs.

The `Post()` function sends data synchronously to blocks and returns `true` if the data was successfully accepted. If the block refuses the data, the function returns `false` and it will not attempt to resend it.

In this example the numbers 0 through 9 are pushed to `actionBlock`. The block takes each value and calls the `Action<T>` that was given at creation. Since, in this example, our action simply prints the received data, the output to the console looks like:

```
Done
0
1
2
3
4
5
6
```

7
8
9

Notice how "Done" was printed first. This is because actionBlock was executed in parallel to the main thread.

ActionBlock<T> Example 2

Basic usage with a delay

```csharp
1  ⬚using System;
2  using System.Threading;
3  using System.Threading.Tasks.Dataflow;
4
5  namespace TPLDataflowByExample
6  {
7      class ActionBlockExample2
8      {
9          static public void Run() {
10
11             var actionBlock = new ActionBlock<int>(n => {
12                 Thread.Sleep(1000);
13                 Console.WriteLine(n);
14             });
15             for (int i = 0; i < 10; i++) {
16                 actionBlock.Post(i);
17             }
18
19             Console.WriteLine("Done");
20         }
21     }
22  }
```

This example is almost identical to example 1 except we are now sleeping for one second before printing the value to the console to simulate a long running action in the block. The output is the same as example 1.

2.1.1.2 TransformBlock<T1,T2>

A `TransformBlock<T1,T2>` is very similar to an `ActionBlock<T>` except it also has an output that you can connect to other blocks (linking blocks will be covered in a later section). It is equivalent to a `Func<T1,T2>` in that it returns a result. Similar to an `ActionBlock<T>`, it takes a function at creation that operates on the input data.

This block contains two buffers, one on the input and one on the output but it is best to think of it as only having a single buffer. Two buffers are needed to ensure that the data is transmitted in the same order as it arrived. The output buffer is used to restore the original ordering of the data. But this is an implementation detail that you should know about but not need to worry about normally.

TransformBlock<T1,T2> Example 1

Receive()

```
1   using System;
2   using System.Threading;
3   using System.Threading.Tasks.Dataflow;
4
5   namespace TPLDataflowByExample
6   {
7       class TransformBlockExample1
8       {
9           static public void Run() {
10              Func<int, int> fn = n => {
11                  Thread.Sleep(1000);
12                  return n * n;
13              };
14
15              var tfBlock = new TransformBlock<int, int>(fn);
16
17              for (int i = 0; i < 10; i++) {
18                  tfBlock.Post(i);
19              }
20
21              for (int i = 0; i < 10; i++) {
```

```
22              int result = tfBlock.Receive();
23              Console.WriteLine(result);
24          }
25
26      Console.WriteLine("Done");
27      }
28    }
29 }
```

In this example we create a TransformBlock<T1,T2> with a function that squares the input value after a one second wait to simulate a long running process.

To extract data from a TransformBlock<T1,T2> (or any block with an output) you use the Receive() method that operates synchronously. If no data is available, the thread will be suspended until data is available. We highlight that fact in this example.

Executing this code should display...

```
0
1
4
9
16
25
36
49
64
81
Done
```

The for loop passes the numbers 0 through 9 to the tfBlock. The function that we passed in at creation time then squares each value and sends the result to the output where we Receive() them.

Notice that for this example "Done" is only printed *after* all the output values have been printed. This is because the Receive() method operates synchronously in the same thread as the for loops.

TransformBlock<T1,T2> Example 2

ReceiveAsync(), Task.Result()

```csharp
1   using System;
2   using System.Threading;
3   using System.Threading.Tasks;
4   using System.Threading.Tasks.Dataflow;
5
6   namespace TPLDataflowByExample
7   {
8       class TransformBlockExample2
9       {
10          static public void Run() {
11              Func<int, int> fn = n => {
12                  Thread.Sleep(1000);
13                  return n * n;
14              };
15
16              var tfBlock = new TransformBlock<int, int>(fn);
17
18              for (int i = 0; i < 10; i++) {
19                  tfBlock.Post(i);
20              }
21
22              // RecieveAsynch returns a Task
23              for (int i = 0; i < 10; i++) {
24                  Task<int> resultTask = tfBlock.ReceiveAsync();
25                  int result = resultTask.Result;
26                      // Calling Result will wait until it has a value ready
27                  Console.WriteLine(result);
28              }
29
30              Console.WriteLine("Done");
31          }
32      }
33  }
```

This example shows how to receive data, asynchronously, from all blocks with outputs using the aptly named ReceiveAsync() method. Since it operates asynchronously, the method does not return a value like the Receive() method does. Instead the ReceiveAsync() method returns a Task<T> that represents the receive operation. Calling the Result() method on the returned Task forces the program to wait until data becomes available essentially making it a synchronous operation like the previous example with the same console output. The next example shows how to create a completely asynchronous receive.

───────────────────────────────

TransformBlock<T1,T2> Example 3

ReceiveAsync(), Task.ContinueWith()

```
1    using System;
2    using System.Threading;
3    using System.Threading.Tasks;
4    using System.Threading.Tasks.Dataflow;
5
6    namespace TPLDataflowByExample
7    {
8        class TransformBlockExample3
9        {
10           static public void Run() {
11               Func<int, int> fn = n => {
12                   Thread.Sleep(1000);
13                   return n * n;
14               };
15
16               var tfBlock = new TransformBlock<int, int>(fn);
17
18               for (int i = 0; i < 10; i++) {
19                   tfBlock.Post(i);
20               }
21
22               Action<Task<int>> whenReady = task => {
23                   int n = task.Result;
24                   Console.WriteLine(n);
25               };
26
27               for (int i = 0; i < 10; i++) {
28                   Task<int> resultTask = tfBlock.ReceiveAsync();
29                   resultTask.ContinueWith(whenReady);
30                   // When 'resultTask' is done,
31                   // call 'whenReady' with the Task
32               }
33
34               Console.WriteLine("Done");
35           }
```

```
36      }
37 }
```

If we modify the previous example slightly, we can receive data from blocks asynchronously. The addition of a continuation with the `ContinueWith()` method allows our main thread to proceed without having to wait for data to be available to read.

A continuation is just something that will be done after the `Task` is completed. In this case our continuation is the `whenReady` action that will print the result to the console.

When run, the example displays…

```
Done
0
1
4
9
16
25
36
49
64
81
```

We again have "Done" printed first since the main thread doesn't have to wait to receive data.

2.1.1.3 Block Configuration

All of the pre-defined blocks in the TPL Dataflow library can be configured by passing an options object to the blocks' constructor. Execution blocks use the `ExecutionDataflowBlockOptions` class, grouping blocks use the `GroupingDataflowBlockOptions` class and buffering blocks use the `DataflowBlockOptions` class. `ExecutionDataflowBlockOptions` and `GroupingDataflowBlockOptions` both inherit from the `DataflowBlockOptions` class (described in the Grouping Blocks section).

2.1.1.4 Execution Block Options

In addition to the options provided by its base class, `ExecutionDataflowBlockOptions` also includes the options, `MaxDegreeOfParallelism` and `SingleProducerConstrained`.

ExecutionDataflowBlockOptions Example 1

MaxDegreeOfParallelism

```
1   □using System;
2   using System.Threading;
3   using System.Threading.Tasks.Dataflow;
4
5   namespace TPLDataflowByExample
6   {
7       class ExecutionDataflowBlockOptionsExample1
8       {
9           static public void Run() {
10
11              var generator = new Random();
12              Action<int> fn = n => {
13                  Thread.Sleep(generator.Next(1000));
14                  Console.WriteLine(n);
15              };
16              var opts = new ExecutionDataflowBlockOptions {
17                  MaxDegreeOfParallelism = 2
18              };
19
20              var actionBlock = new ActionBlock<int>(fn, opts);
21
22              for (int i = 0; i < 10; i++) {
23                  actionBlock.Post(i);
24              }
25
26              Console.WriteLine("Done");
27          }
28      }
29  }
```

Blocks can be configured to operate on more than one piece of data at a time. The default is for each value to be processed one at a time. The MaxDegreeOfParallelism option tells the computer to operate on multiple values at a time in parallel.

This example is a modification of the ActionBlock Example 2. We added a random delay to actionBlock to more closely approximate a real world situation. Running this example shows how the output order of values differs from the input order due to different delays.

On my machine running the example produces...

```
Done
1
0
2
3
4
5
7
6
9
8
```

ExecutionDataflowBlockOptions Example 2

SingleProducerConstrained

```
1   □using System;
2   using System.Diagnostics;
3   using System.Threading;
4   using System.Threading.Tasks.Dataflow;
5
6   namespace TPLDataflowByExample
7   {
8       // http://blogs.msdn.com/b/pfxteam/archive/2011/09/27/10217461.aspx
9       class ExecutionDataflowBlockOptionsExample2
10      {
11          static public void Benchmark1() {
12              var sw = new Stopwatch();
13              const int ITERS = 6000000;
14              var are = new AutoResetEvent(false);
15
16              var ab = new ActionBlock<int>(i => { if (i == ITERS) are.Set(); });
17              while (true) {
18                  sw.Restart();
19                  for (int i = 1; i <= ITERS; i++) ab.Post(i);
```

```
20          are.WaitOne();
21          sw.Stop();
22          Console.WriteLine("Messages / sec: {0:N0}",
23              (ITERS / sw.Elapsed.TotalSeconds));
24        }
25      }
26    static public void Benchmark2() {
27        var sw = new Stopwatch();
28        const int ITERS = 6000000;
29        var are = new AutoResetEvent(false);
30
31        var ab = new ActionBlock<int>(i => { if (i == ITERS) are.Set(); },
32            new ExecutionDataflowBlockOptions {
33                SingleProducerConstrained = true
34            });
35        while (true) {
36            sw.Restart();
37            for (int i = 1; i <= ITERS; i++) ab.Post(i);
38            are.WaitOne();
39            sw.Stop();
40            Console.WriteLine("Messages / sec: {0:N0}",
41                (ITERS / sw.Elapsed.TotalSeconds));
42        }
43      }
44    }
45 }
```

The option SingleProducerConstrained is an optimization for situations where there is only a single block feeding data to another block. The creator of the TPL Dataflow library, Stephen Toub, explains its usage:

Dataflow blocks by default are usable by any number of threads concurrently. While flexible, this also places more synchronization requirements, and therefore cost, on the blocks than might otherwise be necessary. If a block is only ever going to be used by a single producer at a time, meaning only one thread at a time will be using methods like Post, OfferMessage, and Complete on the block, this property may be set to true to inform the block that it need not apply extra synchronization. For blocks that observe this property, you can significantly reduce synchronization overheads by setting this property to true. Right now, only ActionBlock pays attention to this property, but more blocks could in the future as necessary.

(from http://blogs.msdn.com/b/pfxteam/archive/2011/09/27/10217461.aspx)

Using his code (above) for a performance comparison, he measured an `ActionBlock<T>` throughput of 10,942,715 without the `SingleProducerConstrained` option (`Benchmark1()`), and 37,456,691 with the option set (`Benchmark2()`).

2.1.2 Buffering Blocks

Buffering blocks do not modify data passing through them. They exist solely to store or distribute data.

2.1.2.1 BufferBlock<T>

A `BufferBlock<T>` is first-in-first-out (FIFO) data queue that is similar to the `TransformBlock<T1,T2>` except it doesn't change the data passing through it.

BufferBlock<T> Example 1

Basic usage

```
1   □using System;
2   using System.Threading.Tasks.Dataflow;
3
4   namespace TPLDataflowByExample
5   {
6       class BufferBlockExample1
7       {
8           static public void Run() {
9
10              var bufferBlock = new BufferBlock<int>();
11
12              for (int i = 0; i < 10; i++) {
13                  bufferBlock.Post(i);
14              }
15
16              for (int i = 0; i < 10; i++) {
17                  int result = bufferBlock.Receive();
18                  Console.WriteLine(result);
```

```
19              }
20
21              Console.WriteLine("Done");
22          }
23      }
24  }
```

This example shows that you can Post() data to the block's input and use Receive() to extract the data from the output.

2.1.2.2 BroadcastBlock<T>

A BroadcastBlock<T> can send a message to multiple blocks so that they all receive a copy of the original message. Most predefined blocks in the TPL Dataflow library will only send a message to one block, the first one to accept the message. But sometimes we want to process a message in multiple ways.

Another unique feature of the BroadcastBlock<T> is that it does not have an internal buffer. If a new message is received by the BroadcastBlock<T>, it will replace the previous message. If a downstream block does not accept a message, the BroadcastBlock<T> will not attempt to resend it. Only the current message will be transmitted. Any new block linking to a BroadcastBlock<T> will automatically be sent the most current message even if it was not immediately received by the BroadcastBlock<T>.

At construction, the BroadcastBlock<T> takes a function whose purpose is to duplicate the value. Care must be taken with reference types. Multiple blocks trying to mutate a reference type can lead to nasty bugs. The duplication function should perform a deep-copy of all reference types for safety. A good rule-of-thumb with dataflow is to always use immutable values.

BroadcastBlock<T> Example 1

Basic usage

```
1   □using System;
2   using System.Threading.Tasks.Dataflow;
3
4   namespace TPLDataflowByExample
5   {
6       class BroadcastBlockExample1
7       {
8           static public void Run() {
9               var printer1 = MakePrintBlock("printer1");
10              var printer2 = MakePrintBlock("printer2");
11              var bcBlock = new BroadcastBlock<int>(n => n);
12
13              bcBlock.LinkTo(printer1);
14              bcBlock.LinkTo(printer2);
15
16              for (int i = 0; i < 10; i++){
17                  bcBlock.Post(i);
18              }
19
20              Console.WriteLine("Done");
21          }
22
23          static ActionBlock<int> MakePrintBlock(String prefix) {
24              return new ActionBlock<int>(
25                  n => Console.WriteLine(prefix + ": " + n)
26                  );
27          }
28      }
29  }
```

To demonstrate how this block operates we need to link it to two other blocks. See the section on Links for the details but all you need to know now is that messages are sent from one block to another over links.

printer1 and printer2 both print the prefix passed to them at construction followed by the number they receive. Like all the other examples, we send the numbers 0 through 9 to the bcBlock and it duplicates them and transmits the copies to both printer blocks. As we are using a simple value type (int) in this example, our duplication function is just n => n.

The result of running this example is shown below (it may be slightly different when you run it). The printer blocks both receive all the same values and their console output is interleaved.

```
Done
printer2: 0
printer2: 1
printer1: 0
printer1: 1
printer1: 2
printer1: 3
printer1: 4
printer2: 2
printer2: 3
printer2: 4
printer2: 5
printer2: 6
printer2: 7
printer2: 8
printer2: 9
printer1: 5
printer1: 6
printer1: 7
printer1: 8
printer1: 9
```

2.1.2.3 WriteOnceBlock<T>

WriteOnceBlock<T> Example 1

Basic usage

```
1    using System;
2    using System.Threading.Tasks.Dataflow;
3
4    namespace TPLDataflowByExample
5    {
6        class WriteOnceBlockExample1
7        {
8            static public void Run() {
9
10               var woBlock = new WriteOnceBlock<int>(n => n);
11
12               for (int i = 0; i < 10; i++) {
13                   woBlock.Post(i);
14               }
15
16               for (int i = 0; i < 10; i++) {
17                   Console.WriteLine(woBlock.Receive());
18               }
19
20               Console.WriteLine("Done");
21           }
22       }
23   }
```

A `WriteOnceBlock<T>` accepts the only first value it is given and returns that value anytime it is requested. This block is useful for storing constants.

In this example, even though we `Post()` the numbers 0 through 9 to the block, it only accepts the first (zero) and always returns the same even though we call `Receive()` more than once.

2.1.2.4 DataflowBlockOptions

`DataflowBlockOptions` is the parent of both `ExecutionDataflowBlockOptions` and `GroupingDataflowBlockOptions`, therefore the options presented here can also be used with execution and grouping blocks also.

DataflowBlockOptions Example 1

BoundedCapacity, SendAsync()

```csharp
1   using System;
2   using System.Threading;
3   using System.Threading.Tasks.Dataflow;
4
5   namespace TPLDataflowByExample
6   {
7       class DataflowBlockOptionsExample1
8       {
9           static public void Run() {
10
11              Action<int> fn = n => {
12                  Thread.Sleep(1000);
13                  Console.WriteLine(n);
14              };
15              var opts = new ExecutionDataflowBlockOptions { BoundedCapacity = 1 };
16              // Sets the block's buffer size to one message
17
18              var actionBlock = new ActionBlock<int>(fn, opts);
19
20              for (int i = 0; i < 10; i++) {
21                  //Console.WriteLine(actionBlock.Post(i));
22                  actionBlock.SendAsync(i);
23              }
24
25              Console.WriteLine("Done");
26          }
27      }
28  }
```

Every block in TPL Dataflow has an internal buffer that you can control. In this example we set the buffer size to one with the BoundedCapacity option. That means that there is only a single buffer slot inside the block to store incoming data before it starts to process the data. By default, buffers have an unbounded capacity.

 BoundedCapacity may be set to DataflowBlockOptions.Unbounded (-1) to allow for an unbounded buffer size. It also may be set to 1 or greater for a fixed capacity.

 Important!

If BoundedCapacity is 0, an ArgumentOutOfRangeException will be thrown at runtime.

We also had to replace the Post method with SendAsync as a result of the smaller buffer size. To see the reason, uncomment the line with Post and comment the line with SendAsync. The result is...

```
True
False
False
False
False
False
False
False
False
Done
0
```

The Post method pushes the first number, zero, to actionBlock and returns true. When it tries to push the rest of the numbers it is unable to because there's no space left in the block's buffer so it aborts and returns false. Swapping the comments on the Post line and the SendAsync line gives us the expected results.

DataflowBlockOptions Example 2

MaxMessagesPerTask

```
1   using System;
2   using System.Threading;
3   using System.Threading.Tasks.Dataflow;
4
5   namespace TPLDataflowByExample
6   {
7       class DataflowBlockOptionsExample2
8       {
9           static public void Run() {
10
```

```
11        Action<int> fn = n => {
12            Thread.Sleep(1000);
13            Console.WriteLine(
14                n + " ThreadId:" + Thread.CurrentThread.ManagedThreadId
15                );
16        };
17        var opts = new ExecutionDataflowBlockOptions {
18            MaxMessagesPerTask = 1
19        };
20        // Each Task will only process one message
21        // A new task will be created for every new message
22
23        var actionBlock = new ActionBlock<int>(fn, opts);
24
25        for (int i = 0; i < 10; i++) {
26            actionBlock.Post(i);
27        }
28
29        Console.WriteLine("Done");
30        }
31    }
32 }
```

This example uses the MaxMessagesPerTask option to set how many messages each Task will process. Since we set it to one, the Task created by actionBlock will process a single message only and a new Task will be created for every message. The default value is DataflowBlockOptions.Unbounded (-1).

The console output for this example should look like the following (note: the ThreadId will probably be different from one run to the next):

```
Done 0 ThreadId:11
1 ThreadId:12
2 ThreadId:11
3 ThreadId:12
4 ThreadId:11
5 ThreadId:12
6 ThreadId:11
7 ThreadId:12
8 ThreadId:12
9 ThreadId:12
```

While threads are being reused, only one message is being processed at a time.

Limiting the amount of messages per Task can assist in speeding up applications in certain situations. For efficiency reasons, the framework has a pool of threads that it draws from anytime a new Task is created. If a block continuously holds on to a thread because it is processing a constant stream of data, there are less threads to use for other purposes. Creating a new thread takes more time than reusing an old one. So by limiting the amount of messages for a Task, we release the associated thread back to the pool to be used in other areas of our application.

DataflowBlockOptions Example 3

NameFormat

```
1   using System.Diagnostics;
2   using System.Threading.Tasks.Dataflow;
3
4   namespace TPLDataflowByExample
5   {
6       class DataflowBlockOptionsExample3
7       {
8           static public void Run() {
9               var block1 = new BufferBlock<int>(new DataflowBlockOptions {
10                  NameFormat = "Fu"
11              });
12              var block2 = new BufferBlock<int>(new DataflowBlockOptions {
13                  NameFormat = "Bar, Class: {0}, Id: {1}"
14              });
15              Debug.Assert(false);
16          }
17      }
18  }
```

The NameFormat option allows you to define a debug-time name and display format for blocks. The text assigned to the option will be displayed in the debugger. You can use a composite format string, like in the StringBuilder.AppendFormat() method with {0} replaced by the class name and {1} replaced with the block id.

Locals	
Name	Value
⊞ ⬤ block1	Fu, Count=0
⊞ ⬤ block2	Bar, Class: BufferBlock`1, Id: 2, Count=0

2.1.3 Grouping Blocks

Grouping blocks can combine multiple pieces of data to into a container like a List or a Tuple. Sometimes an individual item of data has no meaning on its own. It is only the collection of the data that has meaning. Grouping blocks allow you to gather the data items together and work on the collection as one unit.

Grouping data together can also increase performance because of the reduced synchronization needed to transmit a single group as opposed to all the elements individually.

2.1.3.1 BatchBlock<T>

BatchBlock<T> Example 1

Basic usage

```
1   using System;
2   using System.Threading.Tasks.Dataflow;
3
4   namespace TPLDataflowByExample
5   {
6       class BatchBlockExample1
7       {
8           static public void Run() {
9
10              var batchBlock = new BatchBlock<int>(2);
11
12              for (int i = 0; i < 10; i++) {
13                  batchBlock.Post(i);
14              }
15
16              for (int i = 0; i < 5; i++) {
```

```
17              int[] result = batchBlock.Receive();
18              foreach (var r in result) {
19                  Console.Write(r + " ");
20              }
21              Console.Write("\n");
22          }
23
24          Console.WriteLine("Done");
25      }
26    }
27 }
```

A `BatchBlock<T>` accepts a stream of data and groups them together into a list. The batch size is set at construction.

 ## Important!

The batch size must be 1 or greater or an `ArgumentOutOfRangeException` will be thrown at runtime

In this example we set a batch size of two. So the stream of individual numbers (0 through 9) is grouped together into lists with two elements.

```
0 1
2 3
4 5
6 7
8 9
Done
```

Grouping data together can increase efficiency by reducing the synchronization overhead of transmitting each item separately.

2.1.3.2 JoinBlock<T1,T2>

JoinBlock<T1,T2> Example 1

Basic usage

```
1  using System;
2  using System.Threading.Tasks.Dataflow;
3
4  namespace TPLDataflowByExample
5  {
6      class JoinBlockExample1
7      {
8          static public void Run() {
9              var jBlock = new JoinBlock<int, int>();
10
11             for (int i = 0; i < 10; i++) {
12                 jBlock.Target1.Post(i);
13             }
14
15             for (int i = -9; i < 1; i++) {
16                 jBlock.Target2.Post(i);
17             }
18
19             for (int i = 0; i < 10; i++) {
20                 Console.WriteLine(jBlock.Receive());
21             }
22
23             Console.WriteLine("Done");
24         }
25     }
26 }
```

A JoinBlock<T1,T2> has two inputs (Target1 and Target2) that it combines into a Tuple<T1,T2>. There is also a JoinBlock<T1,T2,T3> to combine three inputs with a resulting output of a Tuple<T1,T2,T3>.

This example produces...

```
(0, -9)
(1, -8)
(2, -7)
(3, -6)
(4, -5)
(5, -4)
(6, -3)
(7, -2)
(8, -1)
```

```
(9, 0)
Done
```

2.1.3.3 BatchedJoinBlock<T1,T2>

A BatchedJoinBlock<T1,T2> is a combination of a JoinBlock<T1,T2> and a BatchBlock<T>. Remember that a JoinBlock returns a tuple of two or three inputs and a BatchBlock<T> returns the input values grouped together into a list. A BatchedJoinBlock combines two or three inputs into a Tuple<T1[],T2[]> or Tuple<T1[],T2[],T3[]>.

While a JoinBlock must have all inputs before it can produce an output, the BatchedJoinBlock can produce an output even if it doesn't have all inputs available. Yet it won't generate an output until the requested batch size it met.

 The batch size is the **total count of elements in all the lists, not a single list.**

 Important!

The batch size must be 1 or greater or an ArgumentOutOfRangeException will be thrown at runtime

---

BatchedJoinBlock<T1,T2> Example 1

Post(), Receive()

```
1    using System;
2    using System.Threading.Tasks.Dataflow;
3
4    namespace TPLDataflowByExample
5    {
6        class BatchedJoinBlockExample1
7        {
8            static public void Run() {
9                var bjBlock = new BatchedJoinBlock<int, int>(2);
10
11               for (int i = 0; i < 10; i++) {
12                   bjBlock.Target1.Post(i);
13               }
14
15               for (int i = 0; i < 10; i++) {
16                   bjBlock.Target2.Post(i);
17               }
18
19               for (int i = 0; i < 10; i++) {
20                   Console.WriteLine(Util.TupleListToString(bjBlock.Receive()));
21               }
22
23               Console.WriteLine("Done");
24           }
25       }
26   }
```

This example posts data to one block at a time, synchronously, resulting in the console output:

```
[0,1] []
[2,3] []
[4,5] []
[6,7] []
[8,9] []
[] [0,1]
[] [2,3]
[] [4,5]
[] [6,7]
[] [8,9]
Done
```

BatchedJoinBlock<T1,T2> Example 2

SendAsync()

```csharp
1   using System;
2   using System.Threading;
3   using System.Threading.Tasks.Dataflow;
4
5   namespace TPLDataflowByExample
6   {
7       class BatchedJoinBlockExample2
8       {
9           static public void Run() {
10              var bjBlock = new BatchedJoinBlock<int, int>(2);
11
12              var delayBlock1 = MakeDelayBlock(1000);
13              var delayBlock2 = MakeDelayBlock(1000);
14
15              for (int i = 0; i < 10; i++) {
16                  delayBlock1.SendAsync(i);
17                  delayBlock2.SendAsync(i - 2 * i); // same number just negated
18              }
19
20              delayBlock1.LinkTo(bjBlock.Target1);
21              delayBlock2.LinkTo(bjBlock.Target2);
22
23              for (int i = 0; i < 10; i++) {
24                  Console.WriteLine(Util.TupleListToString(bjBlock.Receive()));
25              }
26
27              Console.WriteLine("Done");
28          }
29
30          static TransformBlock<int, int> MakeDelayBlock(int maxdelay) {
31              var generator = new Random();
32              return new TransformBlock<int, int>(n => {
33                  Thread.Sleep(generator.Next(maxdelay));
```

```
34              return n;
35           });
36        }
37     }
38  }
```

This example simulates data arriving at the bjBlock asynchronously. We create two TransformBlocks that passes data, unchanged, after a random delay. Both are linked to the bjBlock. The console output for this example should like similar to the following:

```
[0,1] []
[2] [0]
[3] [-1]
[] [-2,-3]
[4] [-4]
[5,6] []
[7] [-5]
[8] [-6]
[9] [-7]
[] [-8,-9]
Done
```

2.1.3.4 GroupingDataflowBlockOptions

GroupingDataflowBlockOptions Example 1

Greedy, Post()

```
1   ☐using System;
2   using System.Threading.Tasks.Dataflow;
3
4   namespace TPLDataflowByExample
5   {
6       class GroupingDataflowBlockOptionsExample1
7       {
8           static public void Run() {
9               var opts = new GroupingDataflowBlockOptions { Greedy = false };
10              var jBlock = new JoinBlock<int, int>(opts);
11
12              for (int i = 0; i < 10; i++) {
13                  if (jBlock.Target1.Post(i)) {
14                      Console.WriteLine("Target1 accepted: " + i);
15                  } else {
16                      Console.WriteLine("Target1 REFUSED: " + i);
17                  }
18              }
19
20              for (int i = 0; i < 10; i++) {
21                  if (jBlock.Target2.Post(i)){
22                      Console.WriteLine("Target2 accepted: " + i);
23                  } else {
24                      Console.WriteLine("Target2 REFUSED: " + i);
25                  }
26              }
27
28              for (int i = 0; i < 10; i++) {
29                  Console.WriteLine(jBlock.Receive());
30              }
31
32              Console.WriteLine("Done");
33          }
34      }
35  }
```

There are two modes of operation for a JoinBlock, greedy (default) and non-greedy. In greedy mode, the block accepts all inputs it is offered even if it can't produce a Tuple. So if the block is offered a value on Target1 only, it will accept the data and wait for data to arrive on Target2 before it produces an output Tuple<T1,T2>. If another value is again offered to Target1, it will again accept it even though it still doesn't have a value on Target2. In non-greedy mode, it will only accept values if both Target1 *and* Target2 have data waiting to be accepted.

Non-greedy mode can be used to prevent dead-locks. Remember that TPL Dataflow uses messages to transmit data. Once a block accepts the message, no other block is also allowed to receive that message. So if we have two `JoinBlock`s with both of their `Target1` linked to the same output and their `Target2` linked to the same (but different from `Target1`) output. One `JoinBlock` could get one of the outputs and the other `JoinBlock` could get the other output. Because neither has enough data to produce an output `Tuple` they are dead-locked. Configuring both of the `JoinBlock`s to non-greedy mode would ensure only one would get both of the outputs and would be able to progress.

This example demonstrates the non-greed behavior. Because we are using the synchronous `Post()` method, when we try to post to `Target1`, in the first `for` loop, it is refused because `jBlock` does not have data available at `Target2` also. It is the same with the second `for` loop because the `JoinBlock` refused all the data we tried to pass to it in the first `for` loop.

The output of this example looks like...

```
Target1 REFUSED: 0
Target1 REFUSED: 1
Target1 REFUSED: 2
Target1 REFUSED: 3
Target1 REFUSED: 4
Target1 REFUSED: 5
Target1 REFUSED: 6
Target1 REFUSED: 7
Target1 REFUSED: 8
Target1 REFUSED: 9
Target2 REFUSED: 0
Target2 REFUSED: 1
Target2 REFUSED: 2
Target2 REFUSED: 3
Target2 REFUSED: 4
Target2 REFUSED: 5
Target2 REFUSED: 6
Target2 REFUSED: 7
Target2 REFUSED: 8
Target2 REFUSED: 9
```

GroupingDataflowBlockOptions Example 2

Greedy, SendAsync()

```
1   ⃞using System;
2   using System.Threading.Tasks;
3   using System.Threading.Tasks.Dataflow;
4
5   namespace TPLDataflowByExample
6   {
7       class GroupingDataflowBlockOptionsExample2
8       {
9           static public void Run() {
10              var opts = new GroupingDataflowBlockOptions { Greedy = false };
11              var jBlock = new JoinBlock<int, int>(opts);
12
13              for (int i = 0; i < 10; i++) {
14                  Task<bool> task = jBlock.Target1.SendAsync(i);
15                  // needed to capture 'i' so we can use it in `ContinueWith`
16                  int iCopy = i;
17                  task.ContinueWith(t => {
18                      if (t.Result){
19                          Console.WriteLine("Target1 accepted: " + iCopy);
20                      } else {
21                          Console.WriteLine("Target1 REFUSED: " + iCopy);
22                      }
23                  });
24              }
25
26              for (int i = 0; i < 10; i++) {
27                  Task<bool> task = jBlock.Target2.SendAsync(i);
28                  // needed to capture 'i' so we can use it in `ContinueWith`
29                  int iCopy = i;
30                  task.ContinueWith(t => {
31                      if (t.Result) {
32                          Console.WriteLine("Target2 accepted: " + iCopy);
33                      } else {
34                          Console.WriteLine("Target2 REFUSED: " + iCopy);
35                      }
36                  });
37              }
38
39              for (int i = 0; i < 10; i++) {
40                  Console.WriteLine(jBlock.Receive());
41              }
42
```

```
43          Console.WriteLine("Done");
44        }
45     }
46 }
```

To get the previous example to run, we need to make a few changes. First we will replace the synchronous Post() with the asynchronous SendAsync(). To determine if the data was accepted by jBlock, we take the Task returned by SendAsync() and add a continuation that is executed after the Task is done.

Now we can still send data to one target at a time with the two for loops. But because SendAsync() will wait until jBlock accepts the data, our example's console output now looks like...

```
Target2 accepted: 9
Target1 accepted: 9
Target2 accepted: 8
Target1 accepted: 8
Target2 accepted: 7
Target1 accepted: 7
Target2 accepted: 6
Target1 accepted: 6
Target2 accepted: 5
Target1 accepted: 5
Target2 accepted: 4
Target1 accepted: 4
Target2 accepted: 3
Target1 accepted: 3
Target2 accepted: 2
Target1 accepted: 2
Target2 accepted: 1
Target1 accepted: 1
Target1 accepted: 0
Target2 accepted: 0
(0, 0)
(1, 1)
(2, 2)
(3, 3)
(4, 4)
(5, 5)
(6, 6)
(7, 7)
(8, 8)
```

```
(9, 9)
Done
```

2.1.4 Block Completion

Block Completion Example 1

Complete()

```csharp
1   using System;
2   using System.Threading;
3   using System.Threading.Tasks.Dataflow;
4
5   namespace TPLDataflowByExample
6   {
7       class BlockCompletionExample1
8       {
9           static public void Run() {
10
11              Action<int> fn = n => {
12                  Thread.Sleep(1000);
13                  Console.WriteLine(n);
14              };
15
16              var actionBlock = new ActionBlock<int>(fn);
17
18              actionBlock.Post(42);
19              actionBlock.Complete();
20              for (int i = 0; i < 10; i++) {
21                  actionBlock.Post(i);
22              }
23              // Even though we send the block all the data it will
24              // only execute once because we tell it to "Complete"
25
```

```
26              Console.WriteLine("Done");
27          }
28      }
29  }
```

You can tell a block to stop processing data with the Complete() method. In this example the value 42 is sent to the block and then it stops because on the next line we call actionBlock.Complete. The console should show...

Done
42

Block Completion Example 2

Complete(), Completion.Wait()

```
1   using System;
2   using System.Threading;
3   using System.Threading.Tasks.Dataflow;
4
5   namespace TPLDataflowByExample
6   {
7       class BlockCompletionExample2
8       {
9           static public void Run() {
10              var block = new ActionBlock<bool>(_ => {
11                  Console.WriteLine("Block started");
12                  Thread.Sleep(5000);
13                  Console.WriteLine("Block ended");
14              });
15
16              block.Post(true);
17
18              Console.WriteLine("Waiting");
19              block.Complete();
```

```
20            block.Completion.Wait();
21            Console.WriteLine("Task done");
22        }
23
24    }
25 }
```

In addition to telling a block to complete, we can also wait until it is done. The Completion() method returns a Task that represents the completion state for the block. A common way to make the current thread pause until the block is done is to call the Wait() method on the returned task.

In this example, block will print "Block started" upon entry, wait five seconds and then print "Block ended". We send a true value to the block just to activate it and then immediately call block.Complete() to tell it should enter the complete state once it is done with what its current job. The main thread is paused until the block completes with the block.Completion.Wait() statement.

The final result of running this example is...

```
Waiting
Block started
Block ended
Task done
```

2.2 Links

Links are the means by which blocks communicate. Block may be connected to zero or more other blocks by using the LinkTo() method either as static member of the DataflowBlock class or an instance method of any block that inherits from the ISourceBlock interface. TPL Dataflow transmits data using message passing.

When multiple blocks are connected to an output, the message is sent to each block in the order they were linked. The first block that accepts the message causes it to be removed from output queue of the source block and no other blocks are offered the same message. The exception to this rule is the BroadcastBlock<T> that is designed to send the message to *all* linked blocks.

When multiple blocks are connected to an input, messages from all links are merged in a time-order fashion and presented to the block's input as if there was only a single input link.

Messages are transmitted in order. It is not possible for a block to extract a message from a link randomly, only the next available message. If a message is unable to be sent, then no other messages can be transmitted along that link and a dead-lock is possible. If you encounter this situation, consider using a BroadcastBlock<T>.

Inside the block messages may be processed out-of-order due to parallelism or by design but a good rule-of-thumb is that messages are processed in-order.

Since links are not a separate entity from blocks in TPL Dataflow, this message passing protocol is controlled by the blocks themselves. Certain blocks, like the BroadcastBlock<T>, may have different message passing procedures. The protocol I outlined above is the general way most blocks handle messages.

Link Example 1

LinkTo()

```
1   using System;
2   using System.Threading.Tasks.Dataflow;
3
4   namespace TPLDataflowByExample
5   {
6       class LinkExample1
7       {
8           static public void Run() {
9               var bufferBlock = new BufferBlock<int>();
10              var printBlock = new ActionBlock<int>(
11                      n => Console.WriteLine(n)
12                  );
13
14              for (int i = 0; i < 10; i++) {
15                  bufferBlock.Post(i);
16              }
17
18              bufferBlock.LinkTo(printBlock);
19
20              Console.WriteLine("Done");
21          }
22      }
23  }
```

This is a simple example showing the most basic and common method of linking two blocks. All of the values from bufferBlock are transmitted to printBlock via the link.

Link Example 2

Multiple Receivers

```
1   ⃞using System;
2   using System.Threading.Tasks.Dataflow;
3
4   namespace TPLDataflowByExample
5   {
6       class LinkExample2
7       {
8           static public void Run() {
9               var printBlock1 = MakePrintBlock("printBlock1");
10              var printBlock2 = MakePrintBlock("printBlock2");
11
12              var bufferBlock = new BufferBlock<int>();
13
14              bufferBlock.LinkTo(printBlock1, n => n % 2 == 0);
15              bufferBlock.LinkTo(printBlock2);
16
17              for (int i = 0; i < 10; i++) {
18                  bufferBlock.Post(i);
19              }
20
21              Console.WriteLine("Done");
22          }
23
24          static ActionBlock<int> MakePrintBlock(String prefix) {
25              return new ActionBlock<int>(
26                  n => Console.WriteLine(prefix + " Accepted " + n)
27              );
28          }
29      }
30  }
```

As a demonstration of how the typical block tries to deliver messages when there are multiple receivers, this example has two blocks (printBlock1 and printBlock2) connected to one bufferBlock that is the source of the data. We added a filter on the link to printBlock1 to only allow even numbers to pass through.

Since printBlock1 was linked first, bufferBlock will try to deliver messages to that block first. The filter predicate blocks all odd numbers from being sent to printBlock1 so bufferBlock then attempts to send them to printBlock2 and succeeds.

Link Example 3

Multiple Sources

```
1   □using System;
2   using System.Threading.Tasks.Dataflow;
3   using System.Threading;
4
5   namespace TPLDataflowByExample
6   {
7       class LinkExample3
8       {
9           static public void Run() {
10              var source1 = MakeDelayBlock(1000);
11              var source2 = MakeDelayBlock(800);
12
13              var printBlock = new ActionBlock<int>(
14                  n => Console.WriteLine(n)
15              );
16
17              for (int i = 0; i < 10; i++) {
18                  source1.Post(i);
19                  source2.Post(i - 2 * i); // negate i
20              }
21
22              source1.LinkTo(printBlock);
23              source2.LinkTo(printBlock);
24          }
25
26          static TransformBlock<int, int> MakeDelayBlock(int delay) {
```

```
27            var generator = new Random();
28            return new TransformBlock<int, int>(n => {
29                Thread.Sleep(generator.Next(delay));
30                return n;
31            });
32        }
33    }
34 }
```

This example shows what happens when a block's input is linked to multiple source blocks. sourceBlock1 and sourceBlock2 will pass the data through them unaltered after a random delay. We fill sourceBlock1 with the positive values 0 through 9 and sourceBlock2 with the negative values 0 through -9 to make it clear where the data is coming from. Both of the source blocks are linked to the input of printBlock that just prints the value of its inputs to the console. From the output of the execution it is clear that the values from both source blocks are merged in time-order at the input of printBlock. The result on my computer looks like...

```
    0
    0
   -1
    1
   -2
    2
   -3
   -4
   -5
   -6
    3
    4
   -7
   -8
   -9
    5
    6
    7
    8
    9
```

_____

Link Example 4

LinkTo() Filter

```
1   ⬚using System;
2   using System.Threading.Tasks.Dataflow;
3
4   namespace TPLDataflowByExample
5   {
6       class LinkExample4
7       {
8           static public void Run() {
9               var sourceBlock = new BroadcastBlock<int>(n => n);
10                  // we use a BroadcastBlock so it will
11                  // discard unused messages
12              var printBlock = new ActionBlock<int>(
13                      n => Console.WriteLine(n)
14                  );
15
16              // Send only even numbers to printBlock
17              sourceBlock.LinkTo(printBlock, n => n % 2 == 0);
18
19              for (int i = 0; i < 10; i++) {
20                  sourceBlock.SendAsync(i);
21              }
22
23              Console.WriteLine("Done");
24          }
25      }
26  }
```

Links can also filter messages that pass through them. The extension method, LinkTo(target,predicate), allows us to assign a predicate function to the link. Every message is passed to the predicate, if it returns true then the messages is sent to the connected block.

TPL Dataflow ensures that messages are processed in order. So if a link filters a message and there are no other links it can be sent to, then the system will dead-lock. To get around that fact, this example uses a BroadcastBlock<T> as the source. Since a BroadcastBlock<T> will send only the most recent message it receives, all filtered messages are simply discarded to prevent dead-lock.

Link Example 5

LinkTo() Filter, NullTarget<T>

```
1   using System;
2   using System.Threading.Tasks.Dataflow;
3
4   namespace TPLDataflowByExample
5   {
6       class LinkExample5
7       {
8           static public void Run() {
9               var sourceBlock = new BufferBlock<int>();
10              var printBlock = new ActionBlock<int>(
11                      n => Console.WriteLine(n)
12                  );
13
14              // Send only even numbers to printBlock
15              sourceBlock.LinkTo(printBlock, n => n % 2 == 0);
16              // A NullTarget discards all received messages
17              sourceBlock.LinkTo(DataflowBlock.NullTarget<int>());
18
19              for (int i = 0; i < 10; i++) {
20                  sourceBlock.SendAsync(i);
21              }
22
23              Console.WriteLine("Done");
24          }
25      }
26  }
```

In the last example we used a `BroadcastBlock<T>` to discard messages that could not be transmitted due to the filter on the link. Yet, often we need to use filtered links from non-BroadcastBlocks. While we could always insert a `BroadcastBlock<T>`, the extra processing will add to the overhead and slow down the program.

This example shows a better way. We add a link after the filtered link that is connected to a `NullTarget<T>` block from the `DataflowBlock` static class. A `NullTarget<T>` discards all messages it receives. Since we add the link after the filtered link, `sourceBlock` will attempt to send all messages to `printBlock` first and all other messages are then sent to the `NullTarget<T>` block. The result of running this example is the same as the previous example.

2.2.1 DataflowLinkOptions

DataflowLinkOptions Example 1

MaxMessages

```
1   using System;
2   using System.Threading.Tasks.Dataflow;
3
4   namespace TPLDataflowByExample
5   {
6       class DataflowLinkOptionsExample1
7       {
8           static public void Run() {
9               var bufferBlock = new BufferBlock<int>();
10              var printBlock = new ActionBlock<int>(n => Console.WriteLine(n));
11
12              for (int i = 0; i < 10; i++) {
13                  bufferBlock.Post(i);
14              }
15
16              var opts = new DataflowLinkOptions { MaxMessages = 5 };
17              bufferBlock.LinkTo(printBlock, opts);
18
19              Console.WriteLine("Done");
20          }
21      }
22  }
```

Links can be configured to only transmit a certain number of messages in their lifetime. When we create a link between two blocks, we can also set its options. This example sets the MaxMessages field in a DataflowLinkOptions object to five. So, even though we attempt to transmit 10 values over the link (the numbers 0 through 9), only the first five will be sent.

DataflowLinkOptions Example 2

Append

```
1    using System;
2    using System.Threading.Tasks.Dataflow;
3
4    namespace TPLDataflowByExample
5    {
6        class DataflowLinkOptionsExample2
7        {
8            static public void Run() {
9                var block1 = MakePrinter("block1");
10               var block2 = MakePrinter("block2");
11
12               var source = new BufferBlock<int>();
13
14               source.LinkTo(block1);
15
16               var opt = new DataflowLinkOptions { Append = false };
17               source.LinkTo(block2, opt);
18
19               for (int i = 0; i < 10; i++) {
20                   source.SendAsync(i);
21               }
22           }
23
24           static ActionBlock<int> MakePrinter(String prefix) {
25               return new ActionBlock<int>(
26                   n => Console.WriteLine(prefix + ": " + n));
27           }
28       }
29   }
```

By default, blocks attempt to transmit messages to the first link that was added. If it is unable to for whatever reason, then the links are tried in order until the message is accepted. Each call to LinkTo() appends a new link to the collection of links. By setting Append = false in a DataflowLinkOptions object and passing it to the LinkTo() method, we can reverse this and prepend the link to the beginning of the collection causing future messages to be sent through this new link first.

In the code above, block1 is linked first and block2 is linked second. But because we call LinkTo with the append option, block2 is added to the front of the collection and it receives all the messages.

3 Using TPL Dataflow

3.1 A Generator Block

While the TPL Dataflow Library comes with almost every block you will need to build your application, there is one type of block I find useful but is absent from the set of predefined blocks the library offers.

A generator block is a source block that continually outputs data. An audio program may need a sine wave generator or a clock program may need to be updated every minute. These are useful in testing dataflow applications by having a generator that continually produces some output that is feed into the blocks under test.

3.2 How Messages are Transmitted

Many factors affect how, when and if messages are transmitted. For the most part, all predefined blocks transmit messages in the same way but some, like `BroadCastBlock` may do things slightly different. My explanation will cover the most common cases and point out the differences where applicable.

Blocks attempt to transmit messages through links in the order they were added.

Most blocks attempt to send messages to only one target block. For those cases, the block must decide in what order the target blocks are offered the message. The default is to offer blocks the message in the order they were added.

Using the `DataflowLinkOptions.Append` configuration can force that a new link is prepended and not appended to the collection of links.

`BroadcastBlocks` and `WriteOnceBlocks` are designed to send messages to all connected blocks so the order they were added is unimportant.

Link filters can block a message before it gets to the block.

If a link was added with a filter predicate and the message causes the predicate to return `true`, then the message is blocked and next link in line is tried.

Links that exceed `MaxMessages` block messages

The `DataflowLinkOptions.MaxMessages` property can limit the total number of messages that a link will transmit over its lifetime. If this limit has been reached, the message is blocked.

Blocks can refuse messages.

If blocks are in the completed state, error state or its internal buffer is full, the block will refuse the message. A `WriteOnceBlock` will refuse all messages except for the first it receives.

Blocks can postpone messages.

Grouping blocks have the option to operate in non-greedy mode – it will only accept a message when all inputs have a message waiting. In this case the block postpones the message. Either another block will accept the message or the block that postponed it can accept it later.

A non-deliverable message can cause a deadlock

TPL Dataflow will always transmit messages in order. For all blocks except for `BroadcastBlock` and `WriteOnceBlock` a message that canât be transmitted causes the block deadlock and wait until it can be delivered. A `DataflowBlock.NullTarget` is useful in this case.

3.3 Runtime Modification

Blocks can be added and removed at runtime. Adding a link at runtime is just calling the `LinkTo()` method as normal. Unlinking a block can be accomplished by using the IDisposable object that is returned when you initially linked the block. Simply call `Dispose()` on the `IDisposable` to remove the link.

Use this ability with caution. With extensive use in various parts of your application you can never be sure what is connected to what and makes debugging frustratingly difficult.

Modifying the delegate used in execution blocks at runtime is not possible. However it is possible to design a delegate that chooses among a few different functions based upon some criteria. Another option is to just replace the whole block by unlinking the old one and linking a new one. But this also changes the order of links and thus messages transmittal will happen in a different order. You'll need to determine on a case by case basis if this will cause problems.

3.4 Maintaining State Inside an Execution Block

In dataflow literature it is often recommended that blocks be stateless. While you should strive for this goal, sometimes it is not possible. Take for example an `ActionBlock` whose only purpose is to take its incoming data and add it to a collection. The most obvious way to implement this is for the block to retain a reference to the collection from one execution to the next.

At creation time, all execution blocks require a function or procedure that is called when the block receives data. Most of the examples in this book use lambdas (a.k.a. anonymous functions) in the creation statement but a lambda cannot retain state from one invocation to the next. The fix is to create a class that contains both the state and the lambda as a method of the class. Before creating the block you will create an instance of the class you just defined and pass the method as a parameter of the block creation statement. The method can access the state held within the object and so the block is able to maintain state.

For safety, this block should not set `MaxDegreeOfParallelism` greater than the default of 1 or you run the risk of multiple threads attempting to update the state at the same time.

3.5 Converting a Stateful Block to be Stateless

It is always possible to convert a stateful block to one that is stateless but it requires a block with multiple inputs and outputs. Since the predefined blocks do not offer this ability you will also have to implement a custom block before you can use this technique.

The concept is simple. Instead of retaining state, you send the current state on an output that is linked to an input of the same block. The block will still have whatever inputs and outputs needed for its normal operation but will now have one additional input and output. Upon execution the block will get the current state and use it for the current set of input values possibly updating the state. Once the block is done, it will send the new state to the output that is linked back to the input so it can use the new state with a new set of values.

4 Dataflow Program Design

4.1 Block Design

4.1.1 Design for Reuse

One of the key aspects of dataflow is the ability to reuse existing blocks. While reusable code has been preached for decades, it was the programming languages themselves that lead to non-reusable code. You don't know if code is truly reusable until you have reused it at least three times. Yet, re-usability is still something we should strive for and dataflow makes it easier.

Dataflow blocks should be free standing units. Do not reference other blocks or anything outside of a block. In one design I have seen, the author needed to ensure that both of the connected block were completed before the subject block performed some operation. He directly set a continuation on the tasks of the two blocks to accomplish his goal. While it solved his problem this time, there is no way he could reuse the block elsewhere.

If you find there is no way to solve your problem without referencing external entities, then maybe they belong inside the block you are designing.

4.1.2 Create Blocks from Scratch only when Necessary

While it is certainly possible to build a new block simply from the core interfaces of TPL Dataflow (IDataflowBlock, ISourceBlock and ITargetBlock) it is rarely necessary. Building new block by using the predefined blocks is much safer.

When building from scratch, you must ensure that the protocols are identical to the predefined blocks. You can think of the predefined blocks to be equivalent to keywords in C#. You use the keywords to build C# applications. Similarly, you use the predefined blocks to build dataflow applications. Creating a new block from scratch is akin to adding a new keyword to C# and as much care must be taken to ensure it operates correctly.

I recommend using the `DataflowBlock.Encapsulate<T1,T2>` method to build a new block with the same interface as the predefined blocks or to create your own, application specific, interface that all of your blocks will conform to. The key is that we don't have to concern ourselves with the details of message passing, threading issues and other details when we don't have to.

4.1.3 Develop Your Own Block Interface

I often find myself developing my own interface that all of the blocks in my application implement. Since the TPL Dataflow library makes no allowances for blocks that have multiple inputs and/or outputs, my interface mostly deals with making it easy to get access to the internal blocks that act as the input and output connections.

Usually I use a dictionary with a key of type string or GUID to store the 'BufferBlock's that are the "ports" of my application specific blocks. All of my blocks implement this interface so that it is consistent throughout the application. I will also wrap predefined blocks in this interface whenever I need to use them alongside my other application specific blocks, again for consistency.

The idea is to create a layer above what is offered by TPL Dataflow to assist in having blocks with multiple inputs and outputs and any other requirements I need for that specific application.

Keep it simple. Don't create a new messaging protocol or a new way to link blocks. Reuse the basic operations that TPL Dataflow offers like `LinkTo` or `SendAsync`.

4.1.4 Careful with Retaining State in Blocks

Blocks that retain state information from one activation to the next should be used carefully when `MaxDegreeOfParallelism` is set to anything more than the default of 1. This is because a single block will have a single state for all threads. If the block is used in a multithreaded manner, there is a danger of multiple threads updating the state at the same time. Additionally, this makes the block less reusable because you have to ensure that all future users of the block understand the dangers of using the block in a multithreaded manner.

4.2 Favor Application Specific Blocks Over Predefined Blocks

For anything more than a trivial use of the TPL Dataflow library, your application should only use blocks that implement your custom interface (as detailed above). Even when you only need a `BufferBlock` you should wrap it in your own interface to maintain consistency.

The TPL Dataflow Library should be thought of as the tools to build your house not the doors and windows that comprise your house. The library was designed to offer the needed abstractions for a variety of dataflow situations. It wasn't designed with your application in mind. Many uses of dataflow require blocks to have many inputs and output, there may be application requirements that some blocks take priority over others or you may want to make it easy to compose new block by using other blocks.

4.3 Avoid Excess Synchronization and Blocks

Every link requires some overhead to send/receive messages. Eliminate unnecessary blocks to reduce the synchronization requirements. A `BufferBlock` feeding into an `ActionBlock` could be redundant depending on the situation. Remember that most predefined blocks contain their own buffer.

While I have preached making small reusable blocks, sometimes it is better to combine the functionality of a few connected blocks into one for the sake of performance. This reduces the amount of synchronization needed to transmit data between the blocks and the number of Tasks needed. First design for re-usability, then if you need to speed things up, only then consider combining blocks.

TPL Dataflow is not designed for very "small" blocks (e.g. a single addition operation). Medium to large blocks (about the size of a typical procedure or larger) give much better performance.

4.4 Dealing with Loops and Cycles

Anytime you have a link from an output of a downstream block to the input of an upstream block, there is a possibility that the dataflow program could run forever without stopping. This is not always a bad thing. Think of dataflow as being similar to electronic circuits. Circuits are designed to operate continuously until the power is turned off. In most engineering disciplines, the best creations are the one that run continuously for long periods of time without faults.

Don't be too concerned about designing dataflow applications that will terminate. If you need to stop them then you can use the Complete() method or a CancellationToken.

This takes a change of attitude for most developers who were taught that programs that do not terminate are wrong. Dataflow is just a different way to think about programming.

4.5 Prevent Large Buffers

You must be mindful of the rate of incoming data to the rate of processing that data in a block. A high rate of incoming data combined with a slow process could create a large backlog of data in the buffer.

To reduce the likelihood of this situation either increase the MaxDegreeOfParallelism or add more blocks to process the incoming data. But remember that these solutions could also cause the data to be returned in a different order than they arrived.

If maintaining order is required, consider using a BatchBlock to group together multiple data items to be processed at one time.

4.6 Data Should be Immutable

Mutable data and parallelism go together like oil and water.

When using mutable data, anytime you have to split data between two blocks you will have to perform a deep-copy of the object. This is very costly in terms of time and memory.

Of course sometimes it is not possible to use immutable data. In those cases you should design your classes to be thread safe. Use blocking collections, never refer to singletons or global variables and ensure that the platform functions you are using are also thread safe.

4.7 Use SingleProducerConstrained if Possible

In the previous chapter we covered how using the `SingleProducerConstrained` option can drastically speed up your applications when a block will only ever have one source block. The creator of the TPL Dataflow Library showed how, in his benchmarks, it was able to increase performance by a factor of 3. As there is no downside to applying this option, you should use it whenever possible.

www.ingramcontent.com/pod-product-compliance
Lightning Source LLC
Chambersburg PA
CBHW080604060326
40689CB00021B/4929